Paris 2024 Olympics Book

A Journey through Olympic History, Essential Facts, and Fascinating Trivias That Will Test Your Knowledge

Jamie Lingard

Copyright © 2024 by Jamie Lingard - All rights reserved.

The content contained within this book may not be reproduced, duplicated or transmitted without direct written permission from the author or the publisher. Under no circumstances will any blame or legal responsibility be held against the publisher, or author, for any damages, reparation, or monetary loss due to the information contained within this book. Either directly or indirectly. You are responsible for your own choices, actions, and results.

Legal Notice: This book is copyright protected. This book is only for personal use. You cannot amend, distribute, sell, use, quote or paraphrase any part, or the content within this book, without the consent of the author or publisher.

Disclaimer Notice: Please note the information contained within this document is for educational and informational purposes only. All effort has been executed to present accurate, up to date, and reliable, complete information. No warranties of any kind are declared or implied. Readers acknowledge that the author is not engaging in the rendering of legal, financial, medical or professional advice.

The content within this book has been derived from various sources. By reading this document, the reader agrees that under no circumstances is the author responsible for any losses, direct or indirect, which are incurred as a result of the use of the information contained within this document, including. But not limited to, -errors, omissions, or inaccuracies.

PHRYGES: THE OFFICIAL PARIS 2024 OLYMPIC MASCOT

Contents

Introduction 7

Legendary Athletes and Iconic Moments 15

The Evolution of the Olympic Games 23

Olympic Records and Superlatives 29

Olympic Trivia Questions 35

True or False Olympic trivia questions 45

Fill-in-the-blank Olympic trivia questions 48

Olympic trivia Answers 53

    Trivia Scorecard 57

Weird and Wacky Olympic Moments 58

Paris 2024: A Global Celebration of Sport 63

Sports and Events to Watch 69

A Visitor's Guide to the Paris 2024 Summer Olympics 77

Appendix A: Paris 2024 Olympic Schedule 85

Appendix B: List of Participating Countries and Athletes 88

Appendix C: Medal Tally 92

Projected Medal Standings................................. 95

Introduction

The Ancient Olympic Games, held every four years in Olympia, Greece, were not merely athletic competitions. They were grand religious festivals honoring Zeus, the king of the gods. The rituals surrounding the Games were deeply intertwined with Greek religious beliefs and practices.

Rituals and Significance:

- **Religious Ceremonies:** The Games began and ended with elaborate sacrifices and offerings to Zeus. Athletes and spectators alike participated in processions, prayers, and other rituals to seek the gods' favor and protection.

- **The Sacred Truce (Ekecheiria):** A period of peace was declared throughout Greece for the duration of the Games, allowing athletes and spectators to travel safely to Olympia. This truce was considered sacred and a violation was punishable by the gods.
- **The Olympic Oath:** Athletes swore an oath to Zeus to compete fairly and uphold the spirit of sportsmanship. This oath emphasized the importance of honor and integrity in competition.
- **Symbolic Rewards:** Victors were crowned with olive wreaths, a symbol of peace and victory. They were celebrated as heroes and often

received additional honors and privileges in their home cities.

Differences from Modern Competitions:

- **Exclusivity:** Unlike the modern Olympics, which are open to athletes of all nations and backgrounds, the ancient Games were initially restricted to freeborn Greek men. Women were not allowed to compete or even watch the Games.
- **Religious Focus:** The ancient Olympics were deeply rooted in religious beliefs and practices. The modern Games, while still retaining some ceremonial elements, are primarily secular sporting events.

- **Limited Scope:** The ancient Games featured a smaller number of sports compared to the modern Olympics. The events were primarily focused on athletics, combat sports, and equestrian competitions.

- **Amateurism:** In ancient times, athletes competed for honor and glory rather than financial gain. The modern Olympics, while upholding the ideal of amateurism for many years, have gradually embraced professionalism and commercialization.

Pierre de Coubertin's Motivations and Goals:

Pierre de Coubertin, a French educator and visionary, was the driving force behind the revival of the Olympic

Games in the late 19th century. He believed that sports could promote international peace, understanding, and cooperation. His motivations included:

- **Educational Reform:** Coubertin saw sports as an essential part of education, promoting physical fitness, discipline, and character development. He hoped the Olympics would inspire young people to embrace athletic pursuits and strive for excellence.

- **International Harmony:** He envisioned the Olympics as a platform for athletes from different nations to compete peacefully and build bridges of friendship. He believed that sports could transcend cultural and political differences.

- **Celebration of Human Potential:** Coubertin saw the Olympics as a showcase for human achievement and the pursuit of excellence. He wanted to inspire people to push their limits and strive for greatness in all aspects of life.

By reviving the Olympic Games, Coubertin sought to create a global movement that would promote peace, education, and human potential. The modern Olympics have largely fulfilled his vision, becoming the world's largest and most prestigious sporting event.

Legendary Athletes and Iconic Moments

Jesse Owens (USA):

- **Personal Story:** An African-American athlete during a time of racial segregation, Owens faced discrimination and prejudice.
- **Challenges:** He had to overcome societal barriers and prove his worth as an athlete despite the racism prevalent in the 1930s.
- **Achievements:** Won four gold medals at the 1936 Berlin Olympics, shattering Adolf Hitler's propaganda of Aryan supremacy.

- **Impact:** Became a symbol of hope and resilience, challenging racial stereotypes and paving the way for future generations of Black athletes.

Wilma Rudolph (USA):

- **Personal Story:** Overcame polio as a child, which left her with a weakened leg and initially unable to walk.
- **Challenges:** Had to endure years of physical therapy and societal doubts about her ability to compete.
- **Achievements:** Won three gold medals in track and field at the 1960 Rome Olympics, becoming the fastest woman in the world.

- **Impact:** Inspired people with disabilities, showing that with determination and perseverance, anything is possible. Became a role model for women in sports.

Muhammad Ali (USA):

- **Personal Story:** Born Cassius Clay, he converted to Islam and changed his name, facing backlash and controversy.
- **Challenges:** Stripped of his boxing title and banned from the sport for refusing to serve in the Vietnam War due to his religious beliefs.
- **Achievements:** Regained his title and became a three-time heavyweight champion, known for his charisma, athleticism, and social activism.

- **Impact:** Transcended boxing, becoming a global icon and a voice for social justice, inspiring generations with his courage and outspokenness.

Jackie Joyner-Kersee (USA):

- **Personal Story:** Grew up in poverty in East St. Louis, facing adversity and limited resources.
- **Challenges:** Battled asthma and injuries throughout her career, but never gave up on her Olympic dreams.
- **Achievements:** Won three gold, one silver, and two bronze medals in heptathlon and long jump across four Olympic Games.

- **Impact:** Empowered women in sports, proving that they could excel in multiple disciplines. Became a role model for young athletes from disadvantaged backgrounds.

Usain Bolt (Jamaica):

- **Personal Story:** Hails from a small town in Jamaica, defying expectations to become a global superstar.
- **Challenges:** Faced skepticism and doubts early in his career due to his unconventional running style and playful personality.
- **Achievements:** Won eight Olympic gold medals in sprinting, setting world records and dominating the sport for a decade.

- **Impact:** Revolutionized sprinting with his speed and showmanship, captivating audiences worldwide and inspiring a new generation of athletes.

These are just a few examples of the many inspiring athletes who have graced the Olympic stage. Their stories of triumph over adversity, dedication to their sport, and impact on society continue to resonate with people around the world. They serve as a reminder that the Olympic Games are not just about winning medals, but also about the human spirit, perseverance, and the pursuit of excellence.

The Evolution of the Olympic Games

The Olympic program has undergone significant changes since the first modern Games in 1896, reflecting evolving cultural attitudes, technological advancements, and the desire to engage new audiences.

Addition and Removal of Sports:

- **Early Games:** The initial program focused on traditional sports like athletics, gymnastics, swimming, and wrestling.
- **Expansion:** Over time, new sports were added, such as basketball (1936), judo (1964), and taekwondo (2000).

- **Removals:** Some sports, like croquet and tug of war, were removed due to lack of popularity or participation.

- **Recent Additions:** The 2020 Tokyo Olympics introduced surfing, skateboarding, sport climbing, and karate, aiming to attract younger viewers.

Debate about Breakdancing:

- **Inclusion in Paris 2024:** Breakdancing, also known as breaking, will debut as an Olympic sport in Paris 2024.

- **Arguments for Inclusion:** Proponents argue that breakdancing is a physically demanding and athletic art form with a global following, particularly among younger generations. It adds diversity and urban culture to the Olympic program.

- **Arguments against Inclusion:** Critics question its legitimacy as a sport and its potential to dilute the traditional Olympic values. They argue that it may be difficult to judge objectively and could lead to commercialization.

Growing Participation of Women:

- **Early Struggles:** Women's participation was limited in the early Olympics. The first female Olympians competed in 1900, but only in a few sports like tennis and golf.

- **Milestones:**
    - 1928: Women's track and field events were introduced.
    - 1984: The first women's marathon was held.
    - 2012: Women competed in all sports for the first time.
- **Challenges:** Despite progress, gender disparities persist. Some sports still have fewer events for women, and there are ongoing debates about equal pay and media coverage for female athletes.

Paris 2024 and Gender Equality:

- **Goal of Gender Balance:** The Paris 2024 Olympics aim to achieve full gender balance, with equal numbers of male and female athletes competing.
- **New Opportunities:** The inclusion of breakdancing and other mixed-gender events will further promote gender equality in the Games.

The evolution of the Olympic program reflects the changing nature of sports and society. The inclusion of new sports like breakdancing and the push for gender equality demonstrate a commitment to adapt and stay relevant to a global audience. However, the debate surrounding these changes highlights the ongoing tension between tradition and innovation in the Olympic movement.

Olympic Records and Superlatives

Here are some of the most astonishing records and statistics across various Olympic sports, along with the stories of athletes who achieved them:

Speed:

- **Usain Bolt (Jamaica):** Holds the world records in the 100m (9.58 seconds) and 200m (19.19 seconds), solidifying his title as the fastest man alive. He achieved these records in the 2009 World Championships, showcasing an unparalleled combination of stride length and frequency.

- **Florence Griffith Joyner (USA):** Her world records in the 100m (10.49 seconds) and 200m (21.34 seconds), set in 1988, remain unbroken. Her electrifying speed and flamboyant style earned her the nickname "Flo-Jo."

Distance:

- **Eliud Kipchoge (Kenya):** Became the first person to run a marathon under two hours (1:59:40) in a special event in Vienna in 2019, although it wasn't an official world record. His official marathon record is 2:01:09.
- **Kenenisa Bekele (Ethiopia):** Holds world records in both the 5,000m (12:37.35) and 10,000m (26:17.53), demonstrating

extraordinary endurance and speed on the track.

Strength:

- **Lasha Talakhadze (Georgia):** The current world record holder in weightlifting, with a combined lift of 492 kg in the +109 kg category. His feats of strength are awe-inspiring, pushing the limits of human capability.

- **Tatiana Kashirina (Russia):** Holds multiple world records in women's weightlifting, showcasing incredible power and technique.

Endurance:

- **Katie Ledecky (USA):** A dominant force in swimming, holding world records in multiple freestyle events, including the 400m, 800m, and 1500m. Her stamina and mental fortitude are unmatched.

- **Kilian Jornet (Spain):** Renowned for his ultramarathon and mountain running achievements, Jornet holds speed records for ascents and descents of some of the world's most challenging peaks.

Other Notable Records and Achievements:

- **Michael Phelps (USA):** The most decorated Olympian of all time, with 28 medals, including

23 gold. His dominance in swimming spanned multiple Olympic Games.

- **Larisa Latynina (Soviet Union):** Holds the record for most Olympic medals won by a woman, with 18 medals in gymnastics across three Olympic Games.

- **Bob Beamon (USA):** His long jump of 8.90 meters at the 1968 Mexico City Olympics shattered the previous world record by 55 centimeters, a feat that many considered impossible at the time.

These are just a few examples of the incredible records and achievements that have been made in Olympic history. The athletes who have pushed the boundaries of human performance serve as an inspiration to us all, showcasing the power of dedication, perseverance, and the pursuit of excellence.

Olympic Trivia Questions

1. In what year were the first modern Olympic Games held?

    (a) 1896

    (b) 1900

    (c) 1924

2. The Olympic rings represent:

    (a) The five continents

    (b) The five oceans

    (c) The five original Olympic sports

3. The Olympic motto "Citius, Altius, Fortius" means:

    (a) Faster, Higher, Stronger

    (b) Braver, Stronger, Faster

(c) Stronger, Together, Forever

4. Which city hosted the 2016 Summer Olympics?

    (a) London

    (b) Rio de Janeiro

    (c) Tokyo

5. Which country has won the most gold medals in Olympic history?

    (a) United States

    (b) Soviet Union/Russia

    (c) China

6. Who is the most decorated Olympian of all time?

    (a) Michael Phelps

    (b) Usain Bolt

    (c) Carl Lewis

7. Which sport is NOT part of the Summer Olympics?

    (a) Badminton

    (b) Curling

    (c) Archery

8. The first Winter Olympic Games were held in:

    (a) St. Moritz

    (b) Chamonix

    (c) Lake Placid

9. Which athlete is known as the "fastest man alive"?

    (a) Usain Bolt

    (b) Carl Lewis

    (c) Jesse Owens

10. The Olympic torch relay always starts in:

(a) Athens

(b) Olympia

(c) Rome

11. The five colors of the Olympic rings are:

(a) Blue, yellow, black, green, and red

(b) Blue, yellow, black, green, and purple

(c) Blue, yellow, black, orange, and red

12. Which country hosted the first-ever Paralympic Games?

(a) Italy

(b) Rome

(c) Greece

13. Who was the first woman to win a gold medal in the Olympic marathon?

(a) Joan Benoit Samuelson

(b) Grete Waitz

(c) Rosa Mota

14. The Olympic flame symbolizes:

(a) Peace and unity

(b) Victory and glory

(c) Strength and perseverance

15. Which country is the birthplace of the modern Olympic Games?

(a) Greece

(b) France

(c) Italy

16. Which athlete is known for her dominance in gymnastics?

(a) Simone Biles

(b) Gabby Douglas

(c) Aly Raisman

17. In which year did women first compete in the Olympic marathon?

(a) 1976

(b) 1984

(c) 1992

18. Which sport is known as the "king of sports"?

(a) Soccer

(b) Athletics

(c) Basketball

19. Who was the first Black athlete to win an Olympic gold medal?

(a) Jesse Owens

(b) John Taylor

(c) Alice Coachman

20. Which city will host the 2024 Summer Olympics?

   (a) Los Angeles

   (b) Paris

   (c) Brisbane

21. Which animal is traditionally associated with the Olympic Games?

   (a) Eagle

   (b) Dove

   (c) Hawk

22. The Olympic Games were canceled three times due to:

   (a) World War I and World War II

   (b) Financial difficulties

   (c) Political disagreements

23. Which country boycotted the 1980 Moscow Olympics?

    (a) United States

    (b) Soviet Union

    (c) China

24. Which sport made its debut in the 2020 Tokyo Olympics?

    (a) Surfing

    (b) Skateboarding

    (c) Both (a) and (b)

25. The Olympic flag has a white background with:

    (a) Six rings

    (b) Five rings

    (c) Seven rings

26. The Paralympic Games are for athletes with:

(a) Physical disabilities

(b) Intellectual disabilities

(c) Both (a) and (b)

27. Which athlete is known for lighting the Olympic cauldron in the 1996 Atlanta Olympics?

(a) Muhammad Ali

(b) Carl Lewis

(c) Jesse Owens

28. Which sport was originally called "mintonette"?

(a) Volleyball

(b) Badminton

(c) Tennis

29. The first Olympic mascot was:

(a) Misha the bear

(b) Waldi the dachshund

(c) Sam the eagle

30. Which sport is known as the "ironman" event?

(a) Triathlon

(b) Decathlon

(c) Pentathlon

True or False Olympic trivia questions

31. The Olympic Games have always been held in the summer. **(True or False)**

32. The Olympic torch is lit using a magnifying glass and sunlight. **(True or False)**

33. A country has won a gold medal in every single Summer Olympic Games. **(True or False)**

34. The first Olympic mascot was introduced at the 1972 Munich Games. **(True or False)**

35. The Olympic Games were originally a religious festival in honor of the god Zeus. **(True or False)**

36. The modern pentathlon consists of five events: fencing, swimming, show jumping, pistol

shooting, and cross-country running. **(True or False)**

37. The first Olympic medals were made of gold. **(True or False)**

38. The longest recorded Olympic torch relay was for the 2008 Beijing Games. **(True or False)**

39. The Paralympic Games and the Olympic Games are always held in the same city. **(True or False)**

40. Cricket was once an Olympic sport. **(True or False)**

47 | Summer Olympics 2024

Fill-in-the-blank Olympic trivia questions

41. The _____ Games are a multi-sport event for athletes with disabilities.

42. The official languages of the Olympic Games are English, French, and the language of the _____ country.

43. The five interlocking rings of the Olympic symbol are a representation of the five _____ of the world.

44. The _____ oath is a solemn promise made by one athlete, one judge, and

one coach on behalf of all participants, affirming fair play and adherence to the rules.

45. The Summer Olympics are held every _____ years.

46. The first modern Olympic champion was James Connolly, who won the _____ jump in 1896.

47. The _____ ceremony marks the end of the Olympic Games, featuring a parade of athletes and the extinguishing of the Olympic flame.

48. The first female athlete to win an Olympic gold medal was Charlotte Cooper, who won in _____ in 1900.

49. The Olympic _____ is a symbol of peace, unity, and the continuation of the Olympic spirit.

50. The Olympic Games have been held in _____ different continents.

51. The _____ are the governing body of the Olympic Movement.

52. The _____ Games were introduced by Pierre de Coubertin to promote peace and international understanding through sport.

53. The _____ rings on the Olympic flag are blue, yellow, black, green, and red.

54. The _____ marathon is a race commemorating the run of Pheidippides from the battlefield of Marathon to Athens.

55. The _____ is awarded to the athlete who best exemplifies the Olympic spirit of sportsmanship and fair play.

56. The _____ ceremony marks the official opening of the Olympic Games, featuring a parade of nations and the lighting of the Olympic cauldron.

57. The Winter Olympics are held every _____ years.

58. The first Winter Olympics were held in _____, France, in 1924.

59. The _____ is a symbol of victory in the ancient Olympic Games.

60. The _____ Olympic Games were the first to be televised.

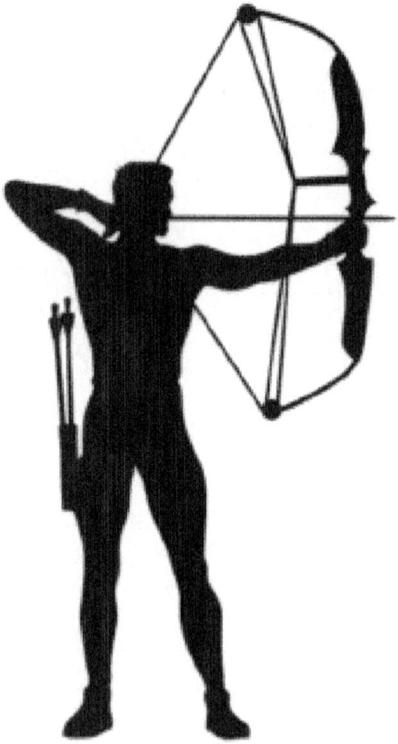

Olympic trivia Answers

1. (a) 1896

2. (a) The five continents

3. (a) Faster, Higher, Stronger

4. (b) Rio de Janeiro

5. (a) United States

6. (b) Usain Bolt

7. (b) Curling

8. (b) Chamonix

9. (a) Usain Bolt

10. (b) Olympia

11. (a) Blue, yellow, black, green, and red

12. (b) Rome

13. (a) Joan Benoit Samuelson

14. (a) Peace and unity

15. (a) Greece

16. (a) Simone Biles

17. (b) 1984

18. (b) Athletics

19. (b) John Taylor

20. (b) Paris

21. (b) Dove

22. (a) World War I and World War II

23. (a) United States

24. (c) Both (a) and (b)

25. (b) Five rings

26. (c) Both (a) and (b)

27. (a) Muhammad Ali

28. (a) Volleyball

29. (b) Waldi the dachshund

30. (a) Triathlon

31. (False)

32. (True)

33. (True - The United States)

34. (True)

35. (True)

36. (True)

37. (False - They were silver)

38. (True)

39. (True)

40. (True - In 1900)

41. (Paralympic)

42. (host)

43. (continents)

44. (Olympic)

45. (four)

46. (triple)

47. (closing)

48. (tennis)

49. (flame)

50. (four)

51. (International Olympic Committee - IOC)

52. (Olympic)

53. (five)

54. (Olympic)

55. (Pierre de Coubertin medal)

56. (opening)

57. (four)

58. (Chamonix)

59. (olive wreath)

60. (1936 Berlin)

Trivia Scorecard

Trivia Master: _____

Date: _____

Total Trivia Score: _____ / 60

When did you get your first answer correctly?

| 1st Try | 2nd Try | 3rd Try | 4th Try | |

Which is your most favorite of all the records?

Weird and Wacky Olympic Moments

Some amusing, surprising, and bizarre anecdotes from Olympic history that highlight the unexpected, controversial, humorous, and unusual events that have occurred over the years:

1. **The Barefoot Marathon Runner:** In 1960, Abebe Bikila of Ethiopia won the marathon barefoot in Rome, setting a world record. He claimed that running barefoot was more comfortable and helped him avoid blisters.

2. **The Human Arrow:** During the 1908 London Olympics, Italian marathon runner Dorando Pietri entered the stadium in first place but was

so exhausted that he collapsed multiple times. He was helped across the finish line but was disqualified for receiving assistance.

3. **The Swimsuit Fiasco:** At the 1904 St. Louis Olympics, the men's swimming competition was held in a murky lake filled with snakes and snapping turtles. One competitor, Fred Lorz, hitched a ride on a boat for part of the race but still claimed victory. He was later disqualified.

4. **The Fosbury Flop:** In the 1968 Mexico City Olympics, high jumper Dick Fosbury revolutionized the sport with his unconventional "Fosbury Flop" technique, jumping backward over the bar. His innovative approach led to a

gold medal and a new standard in high jumping.

5. **The Wrong Anthem:** In a 2004 Athens Olympics medal ceremony, the wrong national anthem was played for the women's 200-meter freestyle winner, Federica Pellegrini of Italy. A technical error led to the playing of the anthem of San Marino instead.

6. **The Ski Jumping Squirrel:** During the 2010 Vancouver Olympics, a rogue squirrel interrupted a ski jumping event, scurrying across the landing area as a competitor was about to jump. Luckily, the athlete was unharmed, and the squirrel became an instant internet sensation.

7. **The Synchronized Swimming Twins:** In the 2000 Sydney Olympics, the identical French twins Virginie and Isabelle Dedieu made history by winning gold in synchronized swimming, a sport that emphasizes precision and coordination.

8. **The Snowboarder's Proposal:** At the 2014 Sochi Olympics, American snowboarder David Wise won gold in the halfpipe and then surprised his girlfriend by proposing to her on live television.

9. **The Mascot Mishap:** During the opening ceremony of the 1988 Calgary Olympics, the inflatable mascot, Hidy the polar bear, deflated

and collapsed in front of the crowd, creating a comical moment.

10. **The Equestrian Refusal:** In the 2004 Athens Olympics, show jumping horse Goldfever refused to jump several fences, costing his rider, Cian O'Connor of Ireland, a gold medal.

These are just a few examples of the many humorous, surprising, and bizarre events that have occurred throughout Olympic history. They demonstrate that the Olympics are not just about athletic achievements, but also about the unexpected moments, human drama, and sheer entertainment that make the Games a global spectacle.

Paris 2024: A Global Celebration of Sport

Paris, the "City of Lights," boasts a rich Olympic heritage and is poised to make history as the second city to host the Summer Games three times. Let's delve into its past Olympic experiences and explore the iconic venues and cultural treasures that will shape the 2024 Games.

A Legacy of Olympic Excellence:

Paris first hosted the Olympics in 1900, a Games marked by innovation and grandeur. Notably, it was the first time women competed in the Olympics. The city's second hosting in 1924 solidified its reputation as a premier sporting destination.

Iconic Venues and Landmarks:

- **Stade de France:** The centerpiece of the 2024 Games, this iconic stadium will host athletics, rugby, and the closing ceremony.

- **Grand Palais:** A masterpiece of Beaux-Arts architecture, this historic landmark will host fencing and taekwondo competitions.

- **Champ de Mars Arena:** With the Eiffel Tower as a backdrop, this temporary venue will showcase beach volleyball.

- **Place de la Concorde:** The largest square in Paris will be transformed into an urban sports park for skateboarding, BMX freestyle, 3x3 basketball, and breaking.

- **The Seine River:** A unique feature of the Paris Games, the Seine will host the opening ceremony, with athletes parading on boats along the river.

- **Château de Versailles:** The opulent palace and gardens will provide a stunning setting for equestrian events.

Cultural Attractions and Artistic Heritage:

Paris is a city steeped in history, culture, and artistic expression. Visitors to the 2024 Games can immerse themselves in a wealth of experiences:

- **World-Renowned Museums:** The Louvre, Musée d'Orsay, and Centre Pompidou house some of the world's most celebrated art collections.

- **Historical Landmarks:** Notre-Dame Cathedral, the Arc de Triomphe, and the Sacré-Coeur Basilica offer glimpses into Paris's rich past.

- **Charming Neighborhoods:** Montmartre, Saint-Germain-des-Prés, and the Marais each possess their own unique character and charm.

- **Culinary Delights:** From Michelin-starred restaurants to cozy cafes and bustling markets, Paris is a culinary paradise.

- **Artistic Expression:** The city's vibrant street art scene, numerous theaters, and music venues showcase the creative energy of Paris.

A Blend of Tradition and Modernity:

Paris seamlessly blends its historical legacy with contemporary innovation. The 2024 Olympics will highlight this unique fusion, using both iconic landmarks and modern sports venues to create a truly memorable Games experience.

By showcasing its rich history, diverse cultural offerings, and commitment to sustainable practices, Paris is poised to deliver an Olympic Games that celebrates the best of sport, culture, and human spirit. The 2024 Games promise to be a transformative event, leaving a lasting legacy for both the city and the Olympic movement.

Sports and Events to Watch

The Paris 2024 Summer Olympics will showcase a diverse array of sports and events, catering to a wide range of interests. Alongside traditional favorites, the Games will introduce new and exciting competitions that promise to captivate global audiences.

New Sports: A Wave of Excitement

- **Surfing:** Held at the picturesque Teahupo'o in Tahiti, surfing will make its Olympic debut. Athletes will be judged on their wave selection, the difficulty of maneuvers, innovation, variety, speed, power, and flow. The unpredictable nature of the ocean and the athleticism of the surfers will make this a thrilling competition.

- **Skateboarding:** Taking place at the Place de la Concorde, skateboarding will feature two disciplines: park and street. Park skateboarding involves performing tricks on ramps and bowls, while street skateboarding focuses on tricks on stairs, rails, and other urban obstacles. This sport's youthful energy and creativity will undoubtedly attract a new generation of Olympic fans.

- **Sport Climbing:** This multi-faceted discipline combines three formats: speed climbing, bouldering, and lead climbing. Speed climbing tests pure speed on a standardized route, bouldering challenges problem-solving skills on shorter walls without ropes, and lead climbing tests endurance and technical ability on taller routes. The combined format will crown a truly versatile champion.

Traditional Favorites: A Showcase of Excellence

- **Athletics:** The track and field events are always a highlight, featuring sprints, middle-distance races, long-distance runs, hurdles, jumps, throws, and multi-event disciplines like the decathlon and heptathlon. The Paris Games will likely see new stars emerge and records broken.

- **Swimming:** The pool events will showcase the world's fastest swimmers competing in freestyle, backstroke, breaststroke, butterfly, and individual medley events. The relays are always exciting, and the open water swimming competition offers a unique test of endurance.

- **Gymnastics:** The artistic gymnastics events, with their combination of grace, strength, and acrobatics, are always a crowd-pleaser. The rhythmic gymnastics competition will feature athletes performing with hoops, balls, clubs, ribbons, and ropes, showcasing elegance and artistry.

Anticipated Highlights and Storylines:

- **Breakdancing:** This new addition to the Olympic program is expected to be a major draw, with its dynamic moves, music, and cultural significance.

- **The Return of Team USA:** After a somewhat disappointing performance in Tokyo, Team USA will be looking to reassert its dominance in many sports, including basketball, swimming, and track and field.

- **The Rise of New Stars:** The Paris Games are likely to introduce a new generation of Olympic heroes, particularly in the newly added sports.

- **The Legacy of Paris:** As the host city, Paris will be keen to showcase its unique charm and culture, creating a memorable Olympic experience for athletes and spectators alike.

With its diverse range of sports and events, the Paris 2024 Summer Olympics promises to be a thrilling and unforgettable celebration of athleticism, human spirit, and global unity.

75 | Summer Olympics 2024

A Visitor's Guide to the Paris 2024 Summer Olympics

Navigating the City of Lights and Experiencing the Games

Ticketing:

- **Official Website:** The official Paris 2024 website is the primary source for purchasing tickets.

- **Authorized Resellers:** Be cautious of unofficial sellers and scams. Only purchase from authorized resellers.

- **Ticket Lottery:** A ticket lottery system may be in place for high-demand events.

- **Hospitality Packages:** These packages offer premium seating and additional perks like exclusive access and dining experiences.

Transportation:

- **Public Transportation:** Paris has an extensive public transportation network, including the metro, buses, and trams. Consider purchasing a Paris Visite travel pass for unlimited travel during your stay.
- **Cycling:** Paris is a bike-friendly city with numerous bike lanes and rental options. Consider exploring the city on two wheels.

- **Taxis and Rideshares:** Taxis and rideshares are readily available, but be prepared for traffic congestion, especially during peak hours.
- **Walking:** Many Olympic venues are located within walking distance of each other, making it easy to explore the city on foot.

Accommodation:

- **Hotels:** Paris offers a wide range of hotels to suit all budgets, from luxury establishments to budget-friendly options. Book well in advance, as demand will be high during the Games.
- **Vacation Rentals:** Consider renting an apartment or house through platforms like Airbnb or Vrbo for a more local experience.

- **Hostels:** If you're on a tight budget, hostels offer affordable dormitory-style accommodations.

Local Attractions:

- **Iconic Landmarks:** Don't miss the Eiffel Tower, the Louvre Museum, Notre-Dame Cathedral, the Arc de Triomphe, and the Sacré-Coeur Basilica.
- **Charming Neighborhoods:** Explore the artistic Montmartre, the intellectual Saint-Germain-des-Prés, and the historic Marais.
- **Cultural Experiences:** Visit the numerous museums and art galleries, catch a show at the

Moulin Rouge, or enjoy a classical music concert at the Sainte-Chapelle.

- **Parks and Gardens:** Relax in the Jardin du Luxembourg, the Tuileries Garden, or the Parc des Buttes-Chaumont.

Navigating the City:

- **Metro:** The Paris metro is the most efficient way to get around the city. Purchase a map or download a metro app for easy navigation.
- **Citymapper:** This app provides real-time transit information and helps you plan your journeys.

- **Walking:** Paris is a pedestrian-friendly city, and walking is a great way to soak in the atmosphere and discover hidden gems.
- **Biking:** If you're comfortable on two wheels, rent a bike and explore the city's many bike lanes.

Food and Beverages:

- **Traditional French Cuisine:** Indulge in classic dishes like croissants, escargot, coq au vin, and crème brûlée.
- **Cafés and Bistros:** Enjoy a leisurely meal or a coffee break at one of Paris's many charming cafés and bistros.

- **Markets:** Visit the local markets for fresh produce, cheese, pastries, and other culinary delights.

- **Street Food:** Sample delicious crepes, falafel, or baguettes from street vendors.

Additional Tips:

- **Learn a few French phrases:** Even a few basic phrases like "bonjour" (hello), "merci" (thank you), and "au revoir" (goodbye) will go a long way in making your experience more enjoyable.

- **Purchase a Paris Passlib':** This pass offers free entry to many museums and attractions, as well as unlimited use of public transportation.

- **Plan your itinerary:** Research the events you want to attend and book your tickets well in advance.

- **Pack for all types of weather:** Paris can experience all four seasons in a single day, so be prepared for anything.

- **Be aware of your surroundings:** As with any major city, be mindful of pickpockets and keep your valuables safe.

With its rich history, vibrant culture, and world-class sporting events, Paris promises to deliver an unforgettable Olympic experience for visitors from around the globe.

Appendix A: Paris 2024 Olympic Schedule

Key Dates:

- **Opening Ceremony:** Friday, July 26th
- **Closing Ceremony:** Sunday, August 11th
- **Competition Dates:** Saturday, July 27th - Sunday, August 11th

Daily Schedule (Subject to change):

The complete Paris 2024 Olympic schedule is available on the official website:

https://olympics.com/en/paris-2024/schedule

The schedule is subject to change and will be updated regularly as the Games approach. Be sure to check the official website for the latest information.

How to Use the Schedule:

- **Search by Sport:** Find your favorite sport and see when and where events are taking place.

- **Search by Date:** See what events are happening on specific days of the Games.

- **Filter by Venue:** See what events are happening at a particular venue.

- **Set Reminders:** Set reminders for events you don't want to miss.

Additional Tips:

- **Plan Ahead:** Many events will be in high demand, so book your tickets as early as possible.

- **Be Flexible:** The schedule is subject to change, so be prepared to adjust your plans if necessary.

- **Arrive Early:** Arrive at the venue well in advance of the start time to avoid delays.

- **Enjoy the Atmosphere:** Even if you don't have tickets to a particular event, soak up the atmosphere in the city and enjoy the festivities.

Appendix B: List of Participating Countries and Athletes

Please note that this is a preliminary list. The final list of participating countries and athletes for the Paris 2024 Olympics will be released closer to the start of the Games.

The Paris 2024 Olympics will welcome athletes from over 200 National Olympic Committees (NOCs) across the globe. Each NOC will send its best athletes to compete in a variety of sports, ranging from traditional events like athletics and swimming to newer additions like sport climbing and breakdancing.

The exact number of athletes per country will vary depending on qualification criteria and the specific sports in which each country excels. Some countries may send a large delegation, while others may have a smaller but equally talented team.

Notable Athletes to Watch:

While the final roster of athletes won't be confirmed until closer to the Games, here are a few notable athletes who are expected to compete in Paris:

- **Simone Biles (USA):** Gymnastics superstar and four-time Olympic gold medalist.
- **Katie Ledecky (USA):** Dominant force in swimming with multiple world records.
- **Shelly-Ann Fraser-Pryce (Jamaica):** Sprinting legend and multiple Olympic gold medalist.

- **Eliud Kipchoge (Kenya):** Marathon world record holder and two-time Olympic champion.

- **Noah Lyles (USA):** Sprinter and rising star in track and field.

- **Yuto Horigome (Japan):** Skateboarding prodigy and Olympic gold medalist.

- **Natalia Grossman (USA):** Sport climbing champion and potential Olympic contender.

- **Caeleb Dressel (USA):** Swimming sensation with multiple Olympic gold medals.

How to Find the Official List:

The official list of participating countries and athletes will be released by the International Olympic

Committee (IOC) closer to the Games. You can find the latest information on the official Paris 2024 website:

https://olympics.com/en/paris-2024

The website will provide detailed information on each country's delegation, including the names of the athletes, their sports, and their competition schedules. You can also find biographies of the athletes, photos, and videos.

Additional Resources:

World Athletics: https://www.worldathletics.org/

FINA (International Swimming Federation): https://www.fina.org/

FIG (International Gymnastics Federation): https://www.gymnastics.sport/site/

IFSC (International Federation of Sport Climbing): https://www.ifsc-climbing.org/

By following the official sources and additional resources listed above, you can stay up-to-date on the latest information regarding the participating countries and athletes at the Paris 2024 Olympics.

Appendix C: Medal Tally

The Medal Tally for the Paris 2024 Olympic Games will be a dynamic and exciting element of the competition. As athletes from around the world strive for gold, silver, and bronze, the medal count will shift and evolve, reflecting the triumphs and achievements of each nation.

The Final Medal Tally will be available on the official Paris 2024 website: https://olympics.com/en/paris-2024

You can also find the updated medal count on various sports news websites and apps throughout the Games.

Projected Medal Standings

While it's impossible to predict the exact outcome, several organizations have released projections based on recent performances and historical trends. According to Nielsen's Gracenote Sports:

- **United States:** Projected to win the most medals overall (123) and possibly lead in gold medals.
- **China:** Expected to finish second in total medals, challenging the United States for the gold medal lead.
- **Great Britain:** Projected to be among the top medal-winning nations.

- **France:** As the host nation, France is likely to see a boost in medal performance.
- **Japan:** Coming off a strong showing in Tokyo, Japan is expected to remain competitive.

These projections are just estimates and the actual results may vary. It's important to remember that every athlete and every event has the potential to surprise and rewrite the medal count.

The Importance of the Medal Tally:

While the medal tally is not the only measure of success at the Olympics, it is a significant and widely followed indicator of national performance. For athletes and countries alike, winning medals is a source of immense pride and recognition.

The medal tally also reflects the level of investment and development in sports within a country. It can inspire future generations of athletes and promote national unity and pride.

Key Factors Influencing the Medal Tally:

- **Athletic Talent and Performance:** Ultimately, the medal tally reflects the skill and dedication of the athletes competing.

- **Team Size:** Countries with larger delegations tend to have more opportunities to win medals.

- **Strength in Certain Sports:** Some countries excel in particular sports, giving them an advantage in those events.

- **Home Advantage:** Host nations often experience a boost in performance due to increased support and familiarity with the environment.

- **Luck and Unexpected Outcomes:** The Olympics are unpredictable, and unforeseen events can significantly impact the medal tally.

By following the medal count, you can track the progress of your favorite athletes and countries, witness thrilling victories, and celebrate the spirit of competition that defines the Olympic Games.

Let's Make Paris Summer Olympics 2024 A Fun Filled One!

Printed in Great Britain
by Amazon